Color and cut out this Easter picture card. Cut out the center hole. Tape a picture of yourself behind the hole. Give the card to a friend.

Happy Easter from your

Cut out this hole. Tape a picture of yourself behind the hole.

"Funny Bunny"!

Signed _____

Date _____

✂ -

Color and cut out the calendar cover-ups. Glue each cover-up to an appropriate calendar date on the next page.

© Carson-Dellosa Publ. CD-8042

CALENDAR

Fill in the month and dates on the calendar. Glue the calendar cover-ups to the calendar. Color the picture.

Sunday	Monday	Tuesday	Wednesday	Thursday	Friday	Saturday

Read the finger play poem. Perform the finger movements as you read the poem again. You may wish to complete the finger puppets on the next page to use with the poem. Color the picture.

The Easter Bunnies
by Katherine Oana

The first fluffy bunny gathered eggs from the hen.
    (Hold up 1 finger)

The second fluffy bunny dyed the eggs in the den.
    (Hold up 2 fingers)

The third fluffy bunny placed the eggs in the baskets.
    (Hold up 3 fingers)

The fourth fluffy bunny said, "A tisket, a tasket."
    (Hold up 4 fingers)

The fifth fluffy bunny said, "There's no time to play."
    (Hold up 5 fingers)

"Let's deliver the baskets on this happy Easter Day!"
    (Move hands as if delivering eggs)

Complete these finger puppets to use with the finger play poem on the preceding page.

Rabbit Finger Puppets

1. Color and cut out each finger puppet on the dotted lines.
2. Glue or tape the tabs together so that the puppet fits around your finger.

Materials: two paper plates, crayons, glue, scissors
1. Cut a paper plate in half.
2. Glue each half section to the top of another paper plate by placing the half sections behind the paper plate. These will be the rabbit's ears. (See example.)

3. Color and cut out all of the pieces on this page.

4. Glue the face to the center of the paper plate. (See example.)

5. Glue the bow tie to the rabbit by placing the bow tie on the bottom rim of the paper plate. (See example.)

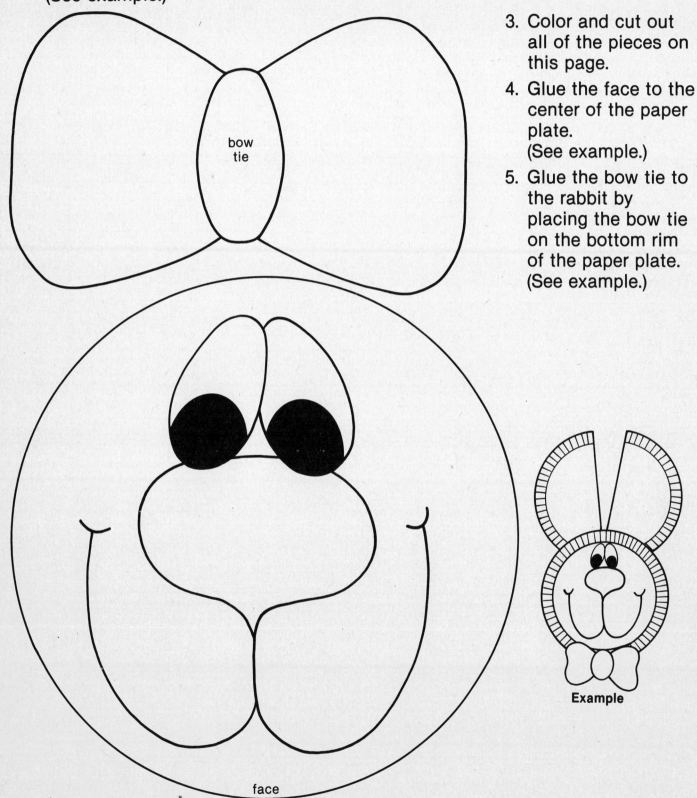

bow tie

face

Example

Girl Rabbit Art Project

1. Color and cut out all of the pieces.
2. Glue the ears to the top of the head by placing the ears behind the head. (See example.)
3. Glue a bow to the bottom of each ear. (See example.)
4. Glue the head to the body. (See example.)
5. Glue the legs to the bottom of the body by placing the legs behind the body. (See example.)

Example

Boy Rabbit Art Project

1. Color and cut out all of the pieces.
2. Glue the ears to the top of the head by placing the ears behind the head. (See example.)
3. Glue the head to the body. (See example.)
4. Glue the bow tie to the body by placing the bow tie under the face. (See example.)
5. Glue the legs to the bottom of the body by placing the legs behind the body. (See example.)

Example

ear

ear

leg   leg

Follow the steps below to draw a rabbit.

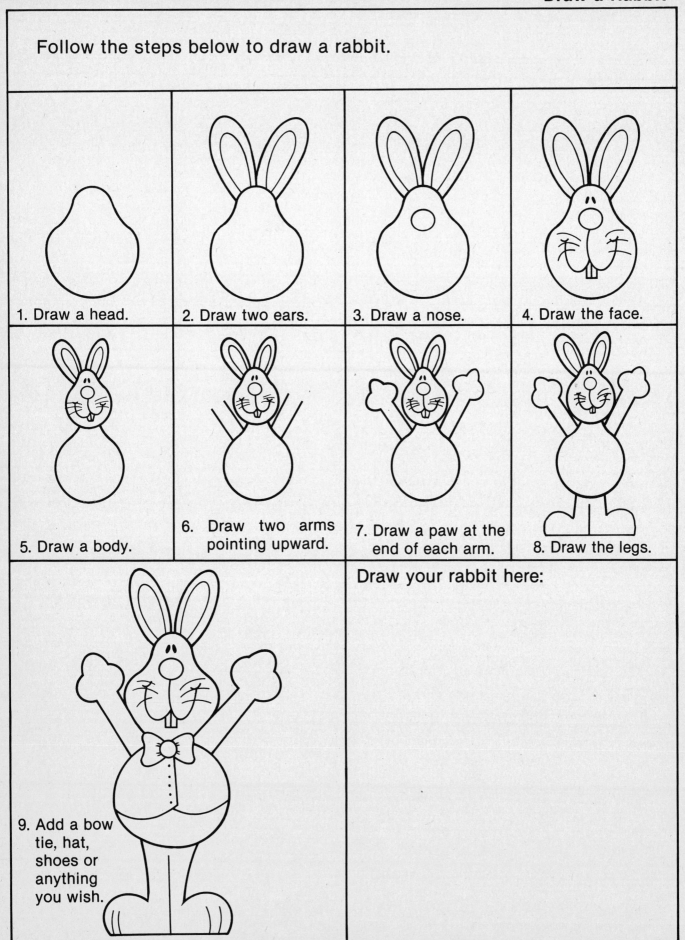

1. Draw a head.

2. Draw two ears.

3. Draw a nose.

4. Draw the face.

5. Draw a body.

6. Draw two arms pointing upward.

7. Draw a paw at the end of each arm.

8. Draw the legs.

9. Add a bow tie, hat, shoes or anything you wish.

Draw your rabbit here:

Read the finger play poem. Perform the finger movements as you read the poem again. You may wish to complete the finger puppets on the following page to use with the poem. Color the picture.

Five Easter Chicks
by Katherine Oana

"No more play. It's time for bed.
Come inside," the Mother Chick said.
(Hand motions "Come inside")

"But first I'll count my chicks and see
If all my darlings came back to me.
(Fingers point as if counting)

Bitsie, Kitsie, and Mitsie, so dear . . .
Witsie and Ditsie; my angels are here.
(Pats each chick on head)

I have the sweetest chicks alive!
My Easter chicks-one, two, three, four, five."
(Hold up 5 fingers)

Complete the finger puppets to use with the finger play poem on the preceding page.

1. Color and cut out each finger puppet.
2. Glue or tape the tabs together so that the puppet fits around your finger.

1. Color and cut out all of the pieces.
2. Glue the eye to the head. (See example.)
3. Glue the beak to the head. (See example.)
4. Glue the head to the body. (See example.)
5. Glue the wing to the body. (See example.)

Easter Chick Art Project

6. Glue the tail to the body by placing the tail behind the body. (See example.)

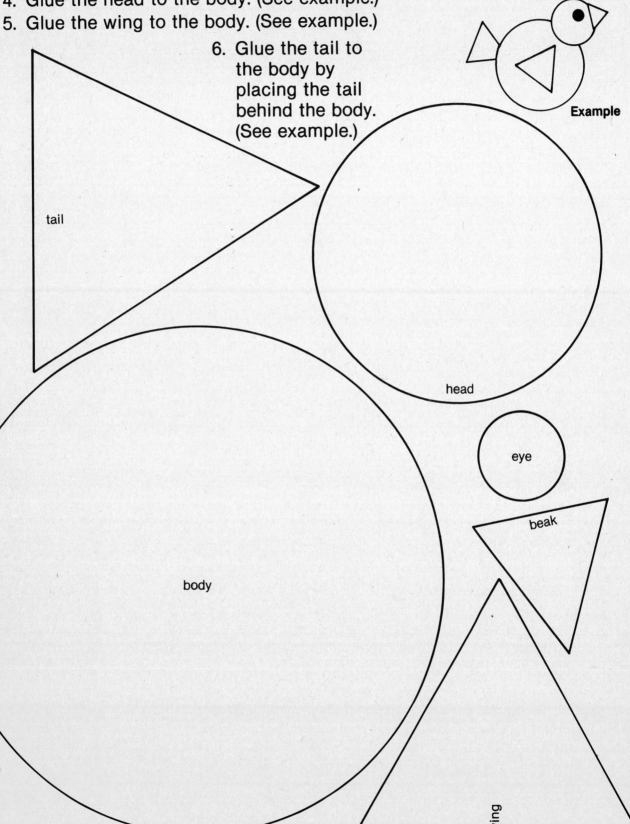

Example

tail

head

eye

beak

body

wing

Color Code · Addition

Solve the problems. Color by number:

5-purple	7-green	9-yellow
6-orange	8-blue	10-red

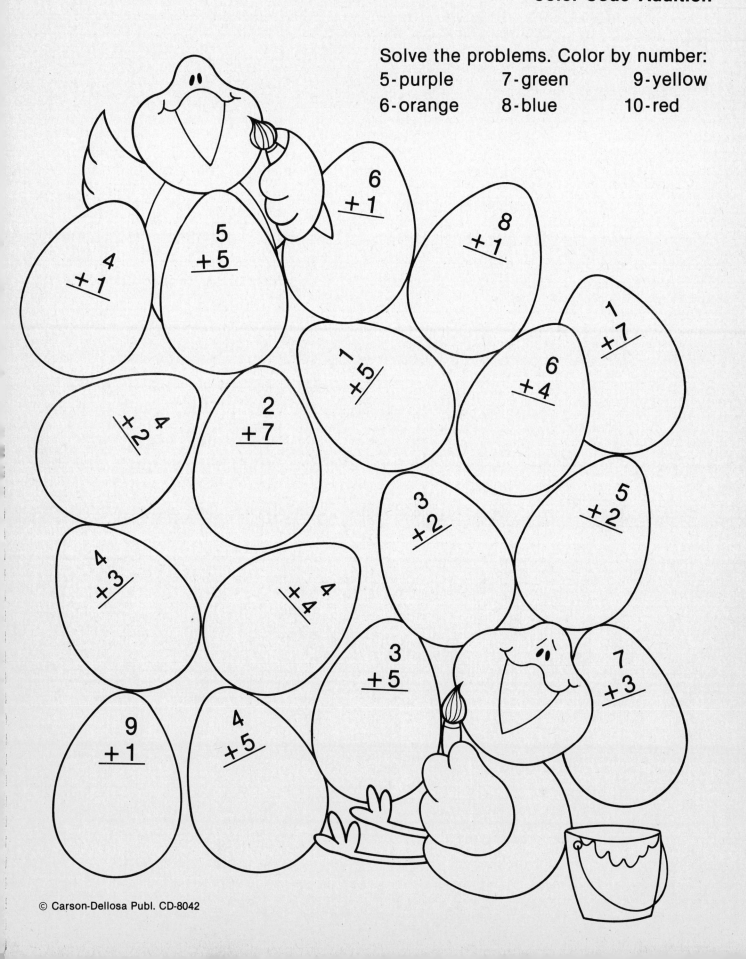

$$4 + 1$$

$$5 + 5$$

$$6 + 1$$

$$8 + 1$$

$$1 + 7$$

$$4 + 2$$

$$2 + 7$$

$$1 + 5$$

$$6 + 4$$

$$3 + 2$$

$$5 + 2$$

$$4 + 3$$

$$4 + 4$$

$$3 + 5$$

$$7 + 3$$

$$9 + 1$$

$$4 + 5$$

© Carson-Dellosa Publ. CD-8042

Easter Finger Play Poem

Read the finger play poem. Perform the finger movements as you read the poem again. You may wish to complete the finger puppets on the next page to use with the poem. Color the picture.

Easter Lambs
by Gail Aemmer

Five Easter lambs; they haven't a care.

They romp and they frolic and jump in the air.

The first lamb is sniffing the bright Easter flowers.   (Hold up 1 finger)

The second is watching the clouds by the hours.   (Hold up 2 fingers)

The third lamb's getting ready for the Easter parade.   (Hold up 3 fingers)

The fourth's eating some of the eggs that he made.   (Hold up 4 fingers)

The fifth lamb's thinking, "Easter's such a nice time,   (Hold up 5 fingers)

To spend playing all day with these great friends of mine!"   (Wiggle all 5 fingers)

Lamb Finger Puppets

Complete these finger puppets to use with the finger play poem on the preceding page.

1. Color and cut out each finger puppet on the dotted lines.
2. Glue or tape the tabs together so that the puppet fits around your finger.

Lamb Art Project

1. Color and cut out all of the pieces.
2. Glue one ear to each side of the head. (See example.)
3. Glue a bow to each ear. (See example.)
4. Glue the head to the body. (See example.)
5. Glue two legs to the front of the body. (See example.)
6. Glue the other two legs to the body by placing them behind the body and the two front legs. (See example.)

Example

Follow the steps below to draw a lamb.

1. Draw the outside shape of the head.

2. Draw the inside shape of the head.

3. Draw a face.

4. Draw two ears.

5. Draw the body.

6. Draw two front legs.

7. Draw two back legs.

8. Decorate your lamb with a bow, bow tie, hat or basket.

Draw your lamb here:

Color Code-Subtraction
Solve the problems.
Color by number:
2-orange   5-yellow
3-red   6-green
4-blue   7-purple
             8-brown

10 − 8 = _____

6 − 1 = _____

10 − 5 = _____

7 − 0 = _____

9 − 6 = _____

9 − 5 = _____

10 − 7 = _____

8 − 3 = _____

9 − 3 = _____

7 − 5 = _____

10 − 2 = _____

8 − 4 = _____

9 − 1 = _____

6 − 4 = _____

6 − 3 = _____

10
− 3

10 − 4 = _____

5 − 0 = _____

9 − 4 = _____

10 − 6 = _____

9 − 7 = _____

9
− 2

7 − 2 = _____

8 − 1 = _____

8 − 5 = _____

8 − 0 = _____

7 − 3 = _____

5 − 3 = _____

8 − 6 = _____

7
− 4

6 − 3 = _____

8 − 2 = _____

Basket Art Project

1. Color and cut out all of the pieces.
2. Glue the rabbit to the top edge of the basket. (See example.)
3. Glue the eggs to the basket by placing the eggs behind the basket. Do not cover up the rabbit. (See example.)
4. Glue the bow to the center of the handle. (See example.)

Example

Happy Easter!

Easter Cards

1. Color and cut out the cards.
2. Fold the cards on the dotted lines.
3. Write a note inside of each card.
4. Sign your name.
5. Give each card to a friend.

Color all of the pieces. Cut out the pictures on the
right and decorate the rabbits below.

Fancy Rabbits